WHAT IS WEATHER?

Sunshine

Miranda Ashwell and Andy Owen

HEINEMANN LIBRARY

First published in Great Britain by Heinemann Library,
Halley Court, Jordan Hill, Oxford OX2 8EJ,
a division of Reed Educational and Professional Publishing Ltd.
Heinemann is a registered trademark of Reed Educational & Professional Publishing Limited.

OXFORD MELBOURNE AUCKLAND
JOHANNESBURG BLANTYRE GABORONE
IBADAN PORTSMOUTH NH (USA) CHICAGO

Designed by David Oakley
Illustrations by Jeff Edwards
Printed and bound in Hong Kong/China

03 02 01 00
10 9 8 7 6 5 4 3 2

ISBN 0 431 03820 1

British Library Cataloguing in Publication Data

Ashwell, Miranda
What is sunshine?. - (What is weather?)
1. Solar radiation - Juvenile literature
I. Title II. Owen, Andy
551.5'271

ISBN 0431038201

Acknowledgements
The Publishers would like to thank the following for permission to reproduce photographs:
Bruce Coleman Limited: Atlantide p26, Dr S Coyne p20, H-P Merten p24; Robert Harding Picture Library: pp7, 19, Robert Francis p14, R Oulds p15, P Robinson p27; Image Bank: I Royd p28; Oxford Scientific Films: D Cox p17, T Jackson p23, S Osolinski p11, M Pitts p18, F Polking/Okapia p5; Pictor International: p6; Planet Earth Pictures: J Lythgoe p10, J MacKinnon p11; Science Photo Library: NASA p10; Still Pictures: M Gunther p22, H Klein p21, NASA p4, T Raupach p25; Telegraph Colour Library: C Ladd p28, F O'Brien p27; Tony Stone Images: T Flach p12.

Cover: F Labhardt, Bruce Coleman Limited.

Every effort has been made to contact copyright holders of any material reproduced in this book. Any omissions will be rectified in subsequent printings if notice is given to the Publisher.

Any words appearing in the text in bold, **like this**, are explained in the Glossary.

Contents

What is the Sun?

The Sun is a star. A star is a burning ball of hot **gas**. The burning gas makes heat and light.

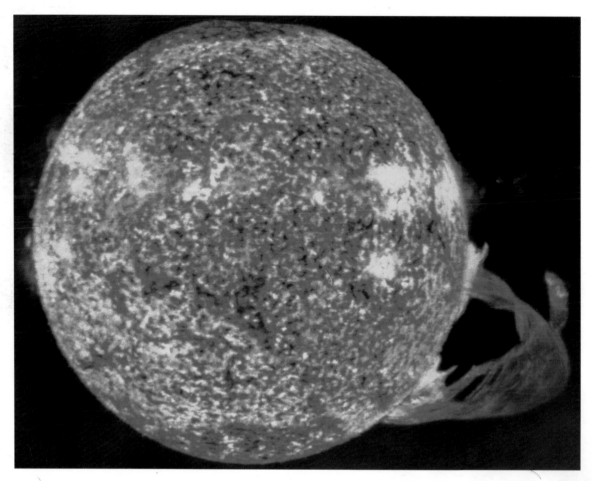

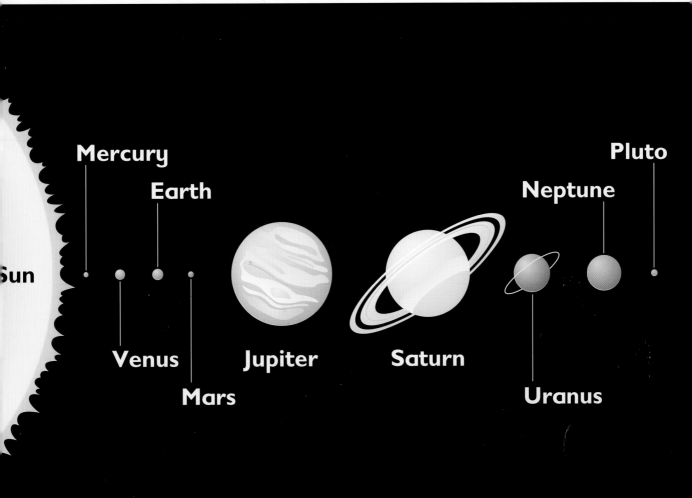

Sun

Mercury

Earth

Venus

Mars

Jupiter

Saturn

Uranus

Neptune

Pluto

The Sun is very many times larger than the Earth where we live. The Earth is a **planet**. It is 150 million kilometres away from the Sun.

Heat from the Sun

Energy from the Sun travels through space. It reaches the Earth and warms the ground.

Air is warmed by the hot ground.
The warm air rises. Warm, rising air
pushed these clouds high into the sky.

Day and night

We have day and night because the Earth turns. On the sunny side of the Earth it is daytime. On the dark side of the Earth it is night-time.

Earth turns this way

It is night here

This is the Sun rising in the morning sky. The Sun seems to move across the sky and go down in the evening. But really the Sun stays still while the Earth is turning.

9

Seasons

Sometimes the part of the Earth where we live is pointing slightly more towards the Sun. The weather is warmer. This is called summer. The weather is colder in winter.

In countries near the **Equator**, the Sun is always nearly overhead and the weather is warm for the whole year.

Long days, short nights

The weather is warmer during the day than at night. This is because the Sun is shining on the other side of the Earth at night.

During the summer, the Sun shines on our part of the Earth for longer each day. Nights are shorter and the weather is warmer.

Shadows

A **shadow** is made when light from the Sun is blocked. Shadows are longest when the Sun is low in the sky. They are shortest when the Sun is high in the sky.

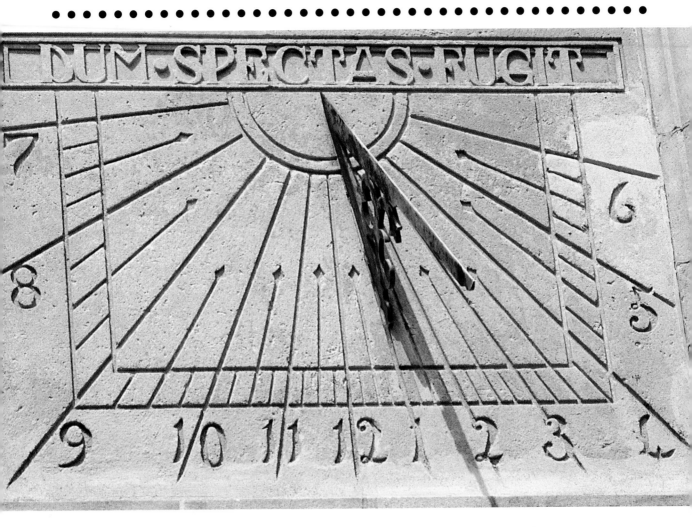

We can use shadows to tell the time.
The metal finger on this **sundial**
makes a shadow. The shadow moves
through the day.

Hot and cold

Heat and light from the Sun are strongest at the **Equator**. This is the hottest part of the world.

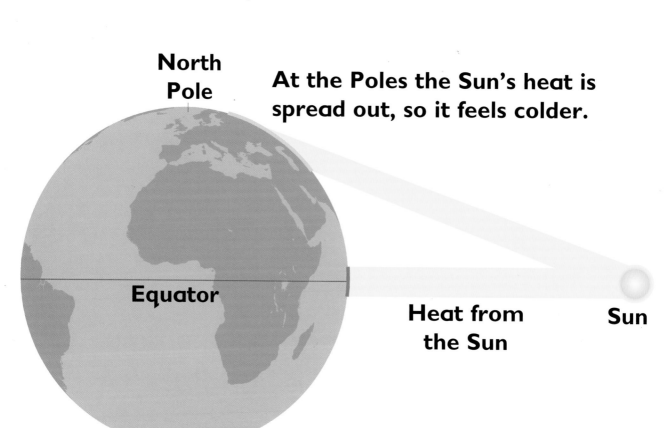

North Pole

At the Poles the Sun's heat is spread out, so it feels colder.

Equator

Heat from the Sun

Sun

The Sun never feels very warm at the
North and South **Poles**. These are
the coldest parts of the world. This is
because the Sun's heat is spread out
at these places.

Plants and the Sun

Green plants use sunlight to make their food. The special green of their leaves can use air and water to change sunlight into food.

Plants grow towards the sunlight. The plants in this forest grow fast and tall in a race to reach the light. Plants with no light will die, because they cannot make their food.

Special plants

Some plants live in the **shadow** of taller plants. They have special leaves to make as much food as possible with only a little light.

Plants that live in very sunny places have special small, waxy leaves that protect the plant. They stop the plant from drying out in the heat of the Sun.

Special animals

Snakes and lizards use heat from the Sun to warm their bodies. Warmth from the Sun makes them more active.

This squirrel lives in a very hot, sunny place. She uses the **shadow** of her large tail to protect herself from the heat of the Sun.

Sun power

These **solar panels** catch energy from the Sun. They turn it into electricity, which we use to heat and light our homes.

Solar panels make all the energy for these electric cars. Most cars use petrol which makes the air dirty. The **solar energy** used by these cars is clean.

Enjoying the Sun

We enjoy resting in the sunshine. Many people go on holiday to warm, sunny places.

In hot countries people often wear
white clothes. White clothes keep us
cooler than dark clothes. They protect
us from the heat of the Sun.

Danger from the Sun

Energy from the Sun can burn our skin and hurt our eyes. On sunny days we protect our skin with special cream. We must also wear a hat and sun-glasses.

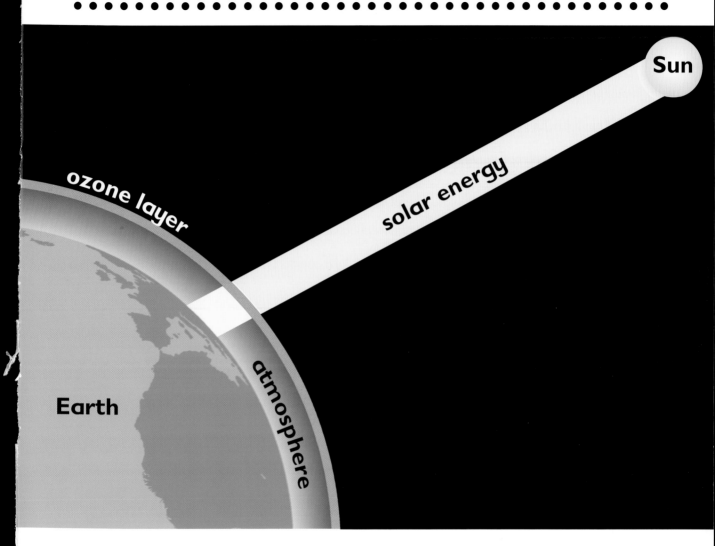

There is a layer of **gases** 24 kilometres above the Earth. These gases block out much of the harmful **solar energy**. This layer is called the **ozone layer**.

It's amazing!

The Sun is 5000 million years old. People think that the Sun will burn for another 5000 million years.

The sunniest place in the world is the Sahara **Desert**. The sun shines for 4300 hours a year, or about 12 hours every day.

In the 1980s, scientists found a hole in the **ozone layer**. It is now even more important that we protect ourselves from the Sun's harmful energy.

Glossary

desert	a place which is very dry, and usually very hot
Equator	a pretend line around the middle of the Earth. It splits the Earth into two halves.
gas	something which is not a solid, like stone, or a liquid, like water. The air is made of many gases.
ozone layer	a layer of gas around the Earth that protects us from the Sun's harmful energy
planet	a large object that circles around a star like the Sun. The Earth is a planet.
poles	the North and South Poles are the two points furthest from the Equator. They are the coldest places on Earth.
shadow	the dark shape made when something blocks light from the Sun
solar energy	heat and light from the Sun
solar panel	turns the Sun's energy into energy we can use
sundial	a type of clock that tells the time with shadows

Index